Prayers

for your

Fasting Journey

Volume 2

Praying Through Strongholds

Vernet Clemons Nettles

Published by: VCNettles Inspirations and Letters, LLC

www.vernetcnettles.com
vernetcnettles@gmail.com

Copyright: January 2026

Scripture from The Holy Bible, New King James Version (NKJV), Copyright 1982 Thomas Nelson.

Cover Design: Elite Book Covers

ISBN: 979-8-9913949-5-6

Printed in the United States

Acknowledgements

First, giving honor to God, who has sustained me through trials, shown me a path, and delivered me to the other side, even though sometimes I lose my way. And, if I'm honest, sometimes I (we) can deliberately get off the path – But I digress.

I am grateful to God that as I write, I am resolving some of my strongholds and beginning to heal. Beginning to let go of heartache and embrace the peace of Jesus in those vacant emotional spaces.

I am also grateful to my family who value what I write enough to read, comment, and challenge my thinking. Your heart is with me and I appreciate you.

I am especially grateful to my friends, who stick by me, read for and with me, but most importantly, they choose me.

Now, thank you to each of the readers. Thank you for trusting your heart enough to purchase this volume. It is my prayer that through the Holy Spirit there is Breakthrough, Release, Grace, and more boundless Love.

Be blessed on this journey.   *Much Love and Peace*

Table of Contents

Additional Scriptures

"And do not be conformed to this world, but be transformed by the renewing of your mind, that you may prove what is that good and acceptable and perfect will of God."

Romans 12:2 NKJV

(This Scripture originally published in the front matter of
***Prayers for Your Fasting Journey** (2023)*

Past and Pass The Strongholds

Each of us can think of a day, a month, or a year when things seemed to turn inside out and upside down. Everything we tried seemed to be almost right and almost wrong. And when we tried to fix it, we broke it. The despair ran deep. Okay, so maybe it was just me.

But that year made me face some of my **strongholds.** I was forced to face some of the issues of life that clung to me, informed my decisions, and berated me when I slipped. Okay so maybe berated is a strong word - but you get it. Sometimes our past rides us like a coat.

It is in those moments that we must dig deep and pray. It is in those moments that we must self-reflect, face our demons, and trade them for God's peace. No, it is not as easy as these few words, but with prayer, time, and patience - it is possible.

So, what's a stronghold? A stronghold is defined as a physical place of refuge and defense, such as a fortress; a spiritual or mental entrenchment of deceptive thoughts, fears, or habits that opposes God's knowledge and truth.

Entrenchment – the process or fact of an attitude, habit, or belief becoming so firmly established that change is very difficult or unlikely.

A **stronghold** is an opportunity for an emotion, a past hurt or action, a fear or habit to deeply embed itself into who we are and block us from experiencing all that God has for us. It creates opposition to what God desires from us. A stronghold creates a personal struggle to see ourselves as God sees us.

I like to use the word **'strangle.'** It's not that I like it – it feels most appropriate. Sometimes our past trauma has such a hold on us, we feel choked and breathless and we are unable to see the goodness that God has for us. But again, maybe it's just me.

This edition of the fasting and devotional journey is designed to help us venture past our hurts. These 21 days may not eliminate all of your personal strongholds or ties that bind. However, use this prayer journey to begin your personal journey of healing and forward momentum.

It's worth it. ***Amen.***

I'm Okay – You're Okay

Transparency - I have spent years willing myself to believe that I am okay. Looking in the mirror and avoiding the deepest gaze. Moving through life, side stepping the deep landmines and choosing the ones that won't shake me to the core.

If this describes you – you, too, could have one or more strongholds.

We choose to avoid the hard emotions. Sometimes, unbeknownst to us, we even wear them like a badge of honor. But if we are honest, we will admit that we have been avoiding some personal truth and living behind our walls – because we presume it is safer.

If that is the case- Let's face it together...

*One More Thing...*Sometimes, we say, "I'm Okay" and we are not. Breathe... It is okay if you are not okay. It is okay to 'take a beat' and just not be okay. It is okay to feel your sadness, to feel your anxiety, to feel your emotions, or to simply feel. It is okay to sit with yourself and wonder.

But when this happens, rest. Feel. Reflect. But do not remain there.

We should strive to recover, to move forward, to come from behind our personal wall – to strive to be better – one day at a time.

If this is also the case – Let's also face it together.

I'm Okay (or not) – You're Okay (or not)

Either way, it is okay.

Because we WILL be okay. **Together.**

Let Us Pray

Disclaimer

This book is written as a ***Prayer Journey*** - a set of prayers to accompany the reader when time is set aside to focus on prayer.

If you choose to fast, here are 21 prayers to help you focus your prayers for ***guidance and revelation.***

This book, however, is not written to promote fasting. Although there are many variations of fasting, ***please consult with your physician(s)*** before beginning any type fast to determine if this is appropriate for your health journey, especially if you have a medical condition.

And if all is well...

Let Us Pray

*(This statement was originally published in **Prayers for Your Fasting Journey** (2023)*

Heart to Heart...

At the top of each Prayer and Reflection page are two hearts. The two hearts represent (1) your heart lifted to God; and (2) my heart praying with yours.

"Two are better than one, Because they have a good reward for their labor. For if they fall, one will lift up his companion...."

Ecclesiastes 4:9-10a NKJV

If you would like to communicate during your Fasting and/or Prayer Journey, I would love to pray with you. Please feel free to email me at vernetcnettles@gmail.com.

(This statement was originally published in ***Prayers for Your Fasting Journey*** *(2023)*

One More Thing...

We vs I   Us vs Me

In my writing, I often pray in the collective. I do so, because I believe that when we pray, we should pray for others and ourselves.

BUT, I encourage you as you read to insert the individual for the collective. Feel the power of your personal journey. Then, pray again in the collective, as we seek the promise for us all.

"Again, I say to you that if two of you agree on earth concerning anything that they ask, it will be done for them by My Father in heaven. For where two or three are gathered together in My name, I am there in the midst of them."

Matthew 18:19-20 NKJV

(This statement was originally published in ***Prayers for Your Fasting Journey*** *(2023)*

"Then I set my face toward the Lord God to make request by prayer and supplications, with fasting, sackcloth, and ashes. And I prayed to the Lord my God, and made confession, and said, "O Lord, great and awesome God, who keeps His covenant and mercy with those who love Him, and with those who keep His commandments,"

Daniel 9:3-4 NKJV

Opening Prayer

Heavenly Father, thank you for all things.

Father, as we move towards a new chapter in our lives. Please continue to help us see those things in our lives that hold us back. Guide us to know that with you, our God, we can begin to break the barriers and strongholds of our lives.

Father, guide our hearts and minds so that every thought is guided by the love of Christ. Father, we have many strongholds and distractions in our lives that desire to conquer us and separate us from you. Father, we ask that you bind those actions and bring us into alignment with your will for our lives.

In Jesus' name, we pray.
Amen.

Prayers

for your

Fasting Journey

VOLUME 2

❦

Praying Through Strongholds

Prayer Day 1

"I will stand my watch And set myself on the rampart, And watch to see what He will say to me, And what I will answer when I am corrected. Then the LORD answered me and said: "Write the vision And make it plain on tablets, That he may run who reads it."

Habakkuk 2:1-2 NKJV

A lot of people love to journal. However, for some of us, (yes, me too) it is a struggle. We whine and say, "Why do I need to write all this stuff down?" Well, this Scripture states, "write the vision." We write for clarity. We write because sometimes our words go directly to our pen, bypassing our mind that would block our secrets. And sometimes we write because we need to see our next steps.

Whether you write for pleasure or purpose, take a few minutes during this prayer time to jot down your thoughts, fears, and moments of overcome – so that you are soon ready to run the race God has for you.

Prayer

Glorious Father, *thank you for the vision and the pen. Father, as we journey during this fasting season, whisper to my heart and my pen, so that I can begin hearing from you and healing from life's circumstances. Father, we need to hear from you. We stand, watch, and pray. In Jesus' name we pray.* **Amen.**

Reflections

What / How are you hearing from God today?

What is your personal prayer for today?

Prayer Day 2

"For though we walk in the flesh, we do not war according to the flesh. For the weapons of our warfare are not carnal but mighty in God for pulling down strongholds, casting down arguments and every high thing that exalts itself against the knowledge of God, bringing every thought into captivity to the obedience of Christ,"

II Corinthians 10:3-5 NKJV

Breathe. We may feel like we are walking through minefields, but if we are honest, much of our struggle is internal - not external. Do we handle our emotions, or do our emotions handle us? Our God is our answer. Sometimes our emotions, our insecurities, our fears, our _____ stand against the promises that God has for us. They keep us from moving forward. So, Breathe. Reflect. And rest in the fact that through God, we can bring those things into obedience of Christ. Our Father can make all things work together for our good. We can overcome our challenges – our strongholds.

Prayer

Heavenly Father, thank you. Father, as we venture into our new chapter, new adventure, or new year, we are grateful that you remind us that we do not wage war as the world does. Father, thank you for reminding us that the struggle is not always what we can see; it is often ideas and hurt(s) that we harbor, that stands against who you have called us to be. Guide our hearts, grant us courage, and help us to believe in who you have called us to become. In Jesus' name we pray. **Amen.**

Reflections

What / How are you hearing from God today?

What is your personal prayer for today?

Courageous Reflections

What is holding you so tightly that you can't move forward?

What pain, sadness, or struggle does your heart revisit?

What are your strongholds?

Thoughts, Prayers, Reflections

Prayer Day 3

"Blessed be the Lord my Rock, Who trains my hands for war, And my fingers for battle— My lovingkindness and my fortress, My high tower and my deliverer, My shield and the One in whom I take refuge, Who subdues my people under me."

Psalm 144:1-2 NKJV

Breathe – a sigh of relief. Thank you, Lord, for training. Scripture states that we should study to show ourselves approved. However, our biblical study is our training. It fortifies us. It strengthens us. It connects us and brings us closer to God. And, as a result of our study and connections to Christ, we can experience more deliverance, more shelter, and more Jesus.

So, breathe a sigh of relief. God is up to something. Not only will people be subdued, but negative emotions and strongholds will also be subdued. Through God, we will bring our strongholds under control.

Prayer

Heavenly Father, *thank you. Thank you for teaching us. Thank you for being our loving kindness, our deliverer, and a place where we are protected and loved. Father, thank you for reminding us that you will train our hands and hearts for the battles of this world. Thank you, Lord. As we venture into our new chapter, we thank you for the comfort in knowing that you are not only our warrior, but you will teach us how to battle. In Jesus' name we pray.* **Amen.**

Reflections

What / How are you hearing from God today?

What is your personal prayer for today?

Prayer Day 4

"The fear of man brings a snare, But whoever trusts in the Lord shall be safe."

Proverbs 29:25 NKJV

The Message Bible says, "The fear of human opinions disables; …" Honestly, sometimes we feel so tied to everyone else's opinion about who we are and what we do. As a little girl, my aunt questioned and chastised my dancing. To this day, I am extremely self-conscious of my dancing until I often trip over my own feet. Although this is a small example, imagine this kind of self-consciousness and self-judgement with other aspects of your life – career choices, relationships, personal decisions, or _____.

The fear of others' opinions and judgement is crippling. What would happen if we took that same energy and purposely invested it in our trust in God. Focus on trusting God every time the negative thoughts creep into our spirits. Instead of always looking for the doubt, let's look for God's assurance. He calls us to walk in Faith. Focus, trust, and be safe in God's Guidance. Try it. Walk it. Break Free.

Prayer

Father God *there are many things we are afraid of as we challenge ourselves to move forward in this new life chapter. Thank you for reminding us that fear is a trap. Fear traps and paralyzes us from moving forward and seeing the blessings you have for us. Father, grant us peace in our hearts as your Word tells us to trust in you and we will be safe. In Jesus' name we pray.* **Amen.**

Reflections

What / How are you hearing from God today?

What is your personal prayer for today?

Prayer Day 5

"For God has not given us a spirit of fear, but of power and of love and of a sound mind."

II Timothy 1:7 NKJV

This Scripture states that God has not given us a spirit of fear. So how do we explain the reality that we get scared and it can sometimes be stifling?

Fear is a human emotion which may be fleeting. But the "spirit of fear" hovers. It clouds our judgment and can cause us to be stuck in our circumstances. The spirit of fear is not of God. God gives; he does not take. God nourishes; He does not drown us in despair. God loves; He does not desire our failure. So, when Scripture states that God has not given us a spirit of fear we should be reminded that we must reach beyond our circumstances to more - more love, more God. Reach because he has not given us a spirit of paralysis; He has given us a spirit to conquer the world.

Prayer

My Lord, thank you for your Word that reminds me to put away my fears as your love is my courage to face what I feel is impossible. Grant me discernment to sift fear from challenge. Guide me to move forward in faith. Grant me grace as I continue on this path. In Jesus' name we pray. **Amen**.

Reflections

What / How are you hearing from God today?

What is your personal prayer for today?

Prayer Day 6

"Therefore I remind you to stir up the gift of God which is in you through the laying on of my hands.

II Timothy 1:6 NKJV

What is something that you love to do or feel called to do? Are you doing it? Do you question whether you should (or should not)? Do you wonder if you are good enough? Do you wonder? So, what are your God-given gifts and talents?

God has given us gifts not only to sustain the Kingdom of Heaven, but to sustain ourselves. Sometimes we feel overwhelmed by the gift or the energy needed for the gift. Have I reached your issues or point of struggle?

Now, read the verse again. God gives us these gifts through His hands, and He calls us to move forward with our gifts. He calls us to grow what he has given us. God wants us to recognize that He has given our gifts to us for us. Not for anyone else. They can't take it, bury it, or shame it away from you. Now, stir up your Gift and use it to build yourself, your joy, and God's Kingdom. Glory to God.

Prayer

Heavenly Father, *thank you for everything – the wonderful gifts and talents you have given. Thank you for your Word that reminds us to stir up the gifts that you have placed in us. Guide us to prepare, learn, and grow our God-given craft. Remind us to put away our fears and embrace your love and strength. Continue to grant us courage to face our challenges. Thank you for your precious gifts of Love, Mercy, and Grace. In Jesus' name we pray.* **Amen.**

Reflections

What / How are you hearing from God today?

What is your personal prayer for today?

Prayer Day 7

"To everything there is a season, A time for every purpose under heaven:"

Ecclesiastes 3:1 NKJV

Some days I wonder if life is ever going to go 'my way.' Some days I wonder if I'm ever going to move from this 'circumstance' that I am in. Some days I face uncertainly, which may turn into fear. Very disheartening. However, Scripture says that there is a purpose for everything.

During these seasons, I have learned to ask God three questions: (1) What do you want me to learn during this season? (2) How can I serve during this season? (3) In my next season, how will these lessons be valuable?

God does not allow trouble without a lesson. Embrace the lesson, not the struggle. Allow the struggle to build more aspects of who you are – your character and your spiritual journey. Then let God show you His wonders – in all things.

Prayer

Father God, thank you. Father, thank you for your true words that tell us that everything in our lives has a season. Thank you for reminding us that there will be a time to hold on and a time to let go. Help us to know when it is time to let go. Give us the courage to release situations and people to you and move forward. Father, we seek direction, wisdom, and strength for our decision and what is to come. And in all things, we seek your Peace. In Jesus' name we pray. **Amen.**

Reflections

What / How are you hearing from God today?

What is your personal prayer for today?

Prayer Day 8

"Nor do they put new wine into old wineskins, or else the wineskins break, the wine is spilled, and the wineskins are ruined. But they put new wine into new wineskins, and both are preserved."

Matthew 9:17 NKJV

Think about it. When you lose weight, you purchase new jeans. You get a new job; you get a new hairstyle. You go on a vacation, you (sometimes) buy a new outfit. Usually, when something grand happens in our lives, we celebrate with something new. Then, why when God is trying to change our perspective and our lives, we revert back to what and who we used to be? Amen or Ouch?

As we are praying to recognize and be released from our strongholds and emotional baggage, let us also pray that God helps us not to return to those spaces, places, people, and emotions. Let us pray that God continues to give us the courage to step out into our newfound freedom – emotionally bag-less. One bag released at a time.

Prayer

Merciful Father, *thank you. We thank you for life and love. Father, thank you for this reminder that when our life situations change, we cannot fill our new life with our old assumptions, emotions, or actions. Father, help us to reframe our thoughts and minds to embrace the new adventures and challenges that you have for us. Help us to embrace our new so that we don't shrink, spill over, and ruin the new challenges and newer opportunities you have prepared. Lord, we need you and we await these new chapters of freedom in our lives. In Jesus' name we pray.* **Amen.**

Reflections

What / How are you hearing from God today?

What is your personal prayer for today?

Prayer Day 9

"Through the Lord's mercies we are not consumed, Because His compassions fail not. They are new every morning; Great is Your faithfulness."

Lamentations 3:22-23 NKJV

We can be stuck. We are stuck in the words we said. We are stuck in the actions we took. We are stuck in the decisions we made. Especially, if what we expected to happen didn't. We worry about the "What If?" Maybe it's just me; because I know people who say, "That was yesterday, this is today." However, I still struggle. Do you?

MyDaddy used to say, "Happy New Year," every day. And he was right. Every day is a new opportunity, a new chance, a new beginning – a new year. An opportunity to do things differently, to get different results, and to reinvent yourself. This is God's Blessings to us. He gifts us new mercies, new compassions, and new mornings each day. So, let's get unstuck. Let's grant forgiveness – for ourselves and others. Let's seek compassion for our missteps. Let's embrace God's faithfulness – morning by morning. Glory to God.

Prayer

Compassionate Father, *thank you for your new mercies every day, every year. Thank you for your compassion and your faithfulness. In this new season, remind us that we can be renewed in you and we can change our directions, because you grant us new beginnings each day. Remind us that we do not have to be stuck. Your mercy can unbind all of our strongholds. In Jesus' name we pray.* **Amen.**

Reflections

What / How are you hearing from God today?

What is your personal prayer for today?

Prayer Day 10

"Do not remember the former things, Nor consider the things of old. Behold, I will do a new thing, Now it shall spring forth; Shall you not know it? I will even make a road in the wilderness And rivers in the desert."

Isaiah 43:18-19 NKJV

Sometimes I hear the hurtful words and smells of the past. They cling to me and upset my momentum. You too or just me? Sometimes, I don't even have to close my eyes, they just echo in my head.

The New Living Translation says, "But forget all that – it is nothing compared to what I am going to do…" Question: If we spend our time re-living what was, when do we have time to anticipate what will be? God has promised us a New Thing. So why not use our energy to prepare for more? Why are we allowing trouble to live rent-free in our hearts and minds? God says that He will make a road in the wilderness. He will make the impossible possible. God has promised a New Thing. So, let's get ready for our miracle. Glory to God.

Prayer

Father God, *thank you. Thank you for prompting us not to remember the old things, the things of our past, the struggles, the bad decisions, the missteps of friends and co-workers, the _____. Your Word promises us renewal, new paths, and opportunities for new choices. Thank you, Lord, for your gift of new chances. In Jesus' name we pray.* **Amen.**

Reflections

What / How are you hearing from God today?

What is your personal prayer for today?

Prayer Day 11

""For if you forgive men their trespasses, your heavenly Father will also forgive you. But if you do not forgive men their trespasses, neither will your Father forgive your trespasses."

Matthew 6:14-15 NKJV

Sometimes we hurt so much, we don't feel like we can forgive the person that hurt us. When I read this Scripture with understanding, my breath stopped for a moment.

We expect that God will forgive us. We relish in the fact that He is a forgiving God. However, God expects that we will forgive those who have caused us hurt and heartbreak. These words are also in The Lord's Prayer: ..." forgive us our debts, as we forgive our debtors."

God calls us to Forgive. So, what do we do? We ask God to show us how to forgive. We ask that He reminds us that forgiveness has more to do with our relationship with Him than with our offender. We accept that forgiveness is not easy, but it is necessary. We focus on Love and pray for Strength.

Prayer

Merciful Father, *thank you for this Word that captures our hearts and causes us to reflect. Father, help us to forgive each other. Help us to understand that, foremost, forgiveness is about our relationship with you. Help us to release our anger and resentment, so that those bitter emotions do not stand in the way of seeing and receiving the blessings you have for us. In Jesus' name we pray.* **Amen.**

Reflections

What / How are you hearing from God today?

What is your personal prayer for today?

Prayer Day 12

"Then Peter came to Him and said, "Lord, how often shall my brother sin against me, and I forgive him? Up to seven times?" Jesus said to him, "I do not say to you, up to seven times, but up to seventy times seven."

Matthew 18:21-22 NKJV

Jesus wants us to forgive. Period. However, forgiveness can be challenging. Sometimes we feel that forgiveness provides a pass. Forgiveness is not a pass; it is an opportunity for the incident not to live rent-free in your spirit, and to restore your peace. Forgiveness provides an opportunity to examine the event, reconcile with self, acknowledge emotions, then let go of the _____ so that you can let God in to heal, comfort, and bless.

Now, 'seventy-times seven' does not mean that you should give yourself over to being mistreated over and over, again. We are expected to forgive; not be harmed. Let us continue to pray that God grants us discernment, so that we can determine who we will allow into our peace. So, pray, forgive, discern, choose. Hallelujah.

Prayer

Compassionate Father, *as we are moving through this new season, teach us to forgive. Father, we expend so much energy being angry instead of enjoying all of the fruit and beauty that you place before us. Father, teach us to forgive and to remember that we all make mistakes. But most importantly, Lord, remind us that we ask you to forgive us, as we forgive others. Guide us to the true meaning of these words. Grant us a clean heart. In Jesus' name we pray.* **Amen.**

Reflections

What / How are you hearing from God today?

What is your personal prayer for today?

Prayer Day 13

"Therefore the kingdom of heaven is like a certain king who wanted to settle accounts with his servants. And when he had begun to settle accounts, one was brought to him who owed him ten thousand talents. But as he was not able to pay, his master commanded that he be sold, with his wife and children and all that he had, and that payment be made. The servant therefore fell down before him, saying, 'Master, have patience with me, and I will pay you all.' Then the master of that servant was moved with compassion, released him, and forgave him the debt."

Matthew 18:23-27 NKJV

"But he owes him," our minds scream. Often, we feel that the bill collectors want an arm, a leg, and our first born. In those moments, we pray for a grace period, for a computer glitch, or a windfall. Now, read this passage again and realize that this is what Jesus does for us – He sees us with compassion and grants us grace. He knows our sins, flaws, and mistakes; yet he is willing to forgive our transgressions. How often do we extend mercy to others? It takes courage to be lenient and forgiving. Can we be like Jesus?

Prayer

Father, *thank you for your mercy and your grace. Thank you for forgiving our sins and giving us new life. Thank you for this example of grace. Remind us, Father, to be kind and forgiving toward each other. Remind us to be lenient in our dealings with others. Father, give us strength and courage to show favor to each other, as you have done for each of us. We are grateful. In Jesus' name we pray.* **Amen.**

Reflections

What / How are you hearing from God today?

What is your personal prayer for today?

Prayer Day 14

""But that servant went out and found one of his fellow servants who owed him a hundred denarii; and he laid hands on him and took him by the throat, saying, 'Pay me what you owe!'" "So when his fellow servants saw what had been done, they were very grieved, and came and told their master all that had been done. Then his master, after he had called him, said to him, 'You wicked servant! I forgave you all that debt because you begged me. Should you not also have had compassion on your fellow servant, just as I had pity on you?'"

Matthew 18:28, 31-33 NKJV

The Pay It Forward Movement still lives on, although seemingly not as loud as previous years. As we are forgiven, it seems that we should further extend forgiveness to others. It's grace. It's kindness. God expects it.

When we earnestly confess our sins to Christ, we are forgiven. So, when others pledge their apologies, why do we still harbor resentment and punishment? Jesus calls us to forgive; then He calls us to pay forgiveness forward. Amen or Ouch? As we are breaking strongholds – forgiving so we can let go – Father, fill our hearts with compassion, we pray.

Prayer

Father, *thank you for your grace. Father, teach us to forgive. We see your awesome examples of forgiveness, and we want to do the same. But sometimes our emotions and feelings get in the way. Father, we see what happened to the unforgiving man when he would not return the kindness given to him. We do not want to be like him. Please continue to pour your love into our hearts. Soften our hearts so that we may see the beauty in forgiveness and the promise you have for us. In Jesus' name we pray.* **Amen.**

Reflections

What / How are you hearing from God today?

What is your personal prayer for today?

Prayer Day 15

"Brethren, I do not count myself to have apprehended; but one thing I do, forgetting those things which are behind and reaching forward to those things which are ahead,"

Philippians 3:13 NKJV

"As far as the east is from the west, So far has He removed our transgressions from us."

Psalm 103:12 NKJV

We speak often of forgiving each other; but we must speak about forgiving ourselves – which is often one of our biggest challenges. It is heartbreaking when we realize that we don't trust ourselves to move forward or make decisions because we haven't forgiven ourselves from past mistakes.

When God calls us to forgive, that luxury is not just for "others," it is also for ourselves. God's Word says to forget those things that are behind us. The Word also says that God removes our transgressions. So, if we are looking back, what should we see? If we continue looking in the rearview mirror, we can't see our blessings up ahead. Amen or Ouch?

Prayer

Gracious and Forgiving Father, *thank you for reminding us that you have forgiven us. Father, teach us to forgive ourselves, to release our missteps and mistakes, our hurts and heartbreaks, our _____, and our _____. Lord, help us to remember that we are not defined by our past mistakes; guide us to leave our struggles with you. Help us to look forward to the future we have with you, to seek the victories and promises that you have for us. Help us, Lord, to release our past failures because they obstruct our view of you and your daily mercies. In Jesus' name we pray.* **Amen**.

Reflections

What / How are you hearing from God today?

What is your personal prayer for today?

Courageous Reflections

Is there someone (or yourself) that you need to forgive?

What happened? Sometimes it helps to journal or talk about it.

You may not be able to forgive right away. How will you work on forgiveness?

PS. *For many of us, forgiveness is not easy or automatic. There is no magic key; I just know that God calls us to be compassionate, merciful, and forgiving. Yes, and Amen.*

Thoughts, Prayers, Reflections

Prayer Day 16

"Bless the Lord, O my soul; And all that is within me, bless His holy name! Bless the Lord, O my soul, And forget not all His benefits: Who forgives all your iniquities, Who heals all your diseases, Who redeems your life from destruction, Who crowns you with lovingkindness and tender mercies, Who satisfies your mouth with good things, So that your youth is renewed like the eagle's."

Psalm 103:1-5 NKJV

When I read this, I breathed a sigh of relief. This Psalm is a celebration of the Lord because he forgives our iniquities. He is not like man, who holds our frailties and mistakes against us. He heals us. He saves us from destruction – from others and ourselves. He renews our hope and strength.

Yet, with all of this goodness, we still choose to hide in corners, drowning in our mistakes, in our inabilities, and in our shame. This Psalm challenges us to be reminded of all of the benefits of walking hand in hand with God. Are we ready to drop the baggage of personal struggle and grab the hand of peace? It is time for each of us to choose.

Prayer

Heavenly Father, thank you for all that you have done and will do. Father God, thank you. We praise your name today and always. Thank you for the forgiveness of our sins, for the healing or our illnesses -physical, spiritual, and emotional. Thank you for the construction and reconstruction of our lives when we are turning things upside down and inside out. Thank you for your loving kindness and your tender mercies that are new every morning. Father, thank you for being our everything! In Jesus' name we pray. **Amen.**

Reflections

What / How are you hearing from God today?

What is your personal prayer for today?

Prayer Day 17

"Then Jesus, again groaning in Himself, came to the tomb. It was a cave, and a stone lay against it. Jesus said, "Take away the stone." Martha, the sister of him who was dead, said to Him, "Lord, by this time there is a stench, for he has been dead four days." Jesus said to her, "Did I not say to you that if you would believe you would see the glory of God?""

John 11:38-40 NKJV

This scripture excites me. How many times do we grieve dreams lost and promises unfulfilled? How many times do we dare not bring those dreams forward, and they remain locked away in the vault of regrets? In this Scripture, Jesus says, "Take away the stone." Then He says, "If you believe...." If we would just believe and trust Jesus, maybe we too could have our treasures and dreams resurrected for "... the Glory of God."

Jesus wants us to release the barriers that block our promises, so that He can resurrect our dreams and promises. He wants us to trust him. Do you? Trust Him?

Prayer

Compassionate Father, *thank you for your empathy and your boldness. Thank you for challenging us to seek beyond what we visibly see with our eyes. Thank you for challenging us to roll away the barriers - beyond the stench of sorrow and broken dreams - to faith that you will fulfill your promises; to faith that you will restore what is locked away, to faith that _____. Glory to God in the Highest. In Jesus' name we pray.* **Amen**.

Reflections

What / How are you hearing from God today?

What is your personal prayer for today?

Prayer Day 18

"Now when He had said these things, He cried with a loud voice, "Lazarus, come forth!" And he who had died came out bound hand and foot with graveclothes, and his face was wrapped with a cloth. Jesus said to them, "Loose him, and let him go.""

John 11:43-44 NKJV

"Speak a word," I like to say. However, these words are specific. Jesus said, "Loose him, and let him go." Jesus has spoken and the expectation is that anything that has bound Lazarus, including death, will release him. Glory!

Lazarus was bound - Strongholds can tie us up. Lazarus was dead. Strongholds can sometimes make us feel that aspects of our life or our dreams are dying or dead. Jesus said, "Lazarus, come forth." We have to be willing to come to Jesus. We have to be willing for Jesus to see us – no more hiding. Our issues must be brought forth. Then Jesus says, "Loose him and let him go." Jesus does not want us to be bound. He does not want us to be constrained by our poor choices, mistakes, and decisions. Are we willing to come forth, so that Jesus can command that we are set free?

Prayer

Heavenly Father, *thank you for all things. Father, thank you for reminding us that when you speak, miracles happen. Father, thank you for reminding us that you are in our corner, that you hear our cries, and answer our call. But also, thank you for reminding us that we must boldly step forth so that we can be set free of our struggles. Thank you, Jesus, for being willing. In Jesus' name we pray.* **Amen.**

Reflections

What / How are you hearing from God today?

What is your personal prayer for today?

Prayer Day 19

"Be sober, be vigilant; because your adversary the devil walks about like a roaring lion, seeking whom he may devour. Resist him, steadfast in the faith, knowing that the same sufferings are experienced by your brotherhood in the world."

I Peter 5:8-9 NKJV

Reread the last phrase of this Scripture. The second time I read it, I heard, "You are not alone." We spend a lot of time suffering in silence. We don't often share our sorrows or our struggles. We hold our cards close expecting that no one else is having the same struggles or no one will understand how we feel. Amen or Ouch?

However, as we lean into God's grace and mercy, He strengthens us during our trials. We should seek to grow closer to God as we seek his counsel. Additionally, as we are comforted in God's grace, we become equipped to comfort, support, and teach others. On Day 7, we asked what we should learn during our struggle. Now, we must ask, "How do we use what we have learned to help someone else?" When we help others, we grow more in grace.

Prayer

Glorious Father, thank you. Thank you for a Word of encouragement to resist, to be steadfast, and to have faith. Thank you reminding us that suffering is not just something that happens to me - that I am not the only one who has challenges. The struggles in life are universal throughout the brotherhood. Father, you have called us to be a brotherhood and sisterhood of faith. Father, teach us to share our burdens - not for attention, but for collective healing. In Jesus' name we pray. **Amen.**

PS: Father, as we share our burdens, teach us to be compassionate when listening, and silent when asked by others. Teach us to be trustworthy listeners. We pray and say thank you. **Amen.**

Reflections

What / How are you hearing from God today?

What is your personal prayer for today?

Prayer Day 20

"Now the Lord is the Spirit; and where the Spirit of the Lord is, there is liberty."

II Corinthians 3:17 NKJV

"Stand fast therefore in the liberty by which Christ has made us free, and do not be entangled again with a yoke of bondage."

Galatians 5:1 NKJV

July 4th is not the only Independence Day in our lives. Our Independence – our Liberty – is connected to each day that we live and love in Christ. Each day that we invite the Spirit of the Lord into our lives, we have Freedom. We have Deliverance. We have Liberty.

We are free from the bondage of other opinions. We are free from crippling mistakes. We are free from hopelessness and despair. In Christ, we are Free to be healed and not permanently wounded; free to live out loud, free to love boldly. We are free from the criticism and scorn of those who want us to fail. We are free of _____. We are free to break free from those things that strangle us from all of God's promises. His answers are Yes and Amen.

Prayer

Majestic and Glorious Father, thank you for life, liberty, and the pursuit of happiness. Thank you for your Word that reminds us that Christ has made us free. Thank you for reminding us that we do not have to remain entangled in the bondage of despair, hopelessness, _____, or _____. Please, Lord, pour into us your Spirit so that may become more and more like you. Guide our hearts to understand that your Freedom allows us to love ourselves and others in sincerity and truth. Thank you for reminding us that when your spirit dwells within us, there is freedom. Come, Holy Spirit, reside in my heart. In Jesus' name we pray. **Amen.**

Reflections

What / How are you hearing from God today?

What is your personal prayer for today?

Courageous Reflections

What have you realized about yourself and your strongholds / struggles?

How have your strongholds / struggles created stumbling blocks or barriers in your life?

What is your plan or path forward to continue reconciling and praying concerning your strongholds / struggles?

Thoughts, Prayers, Reflections

Prayer Day 21

"The Lord is good, A stronghold in the day of trouble; And He knows those who trust in Him."

Nahum 1:7 NKJV

We have spent 21 days praying to break strongholds in our lives. However, The Lord and His Goodness is the only Stronghold I don't want to be released from. This is the only fortress I want to be hidden in. This the only safe place I want to rest in – My Stronghold - My Savior – My Comfort and Hope.

I want to know that in times of trouble, God will hide me. I want to know that when I am afraid, God will comfort me. I want God to know that I trust Him, that I believe in His Promises for my life, and I believe that He is an ever-present source of help, joy, and love.

It was stated earlier that one of the definitions of stronghold was a place of refuge and defense. God is our place of refuge – our place of safety and shelter. However, we must believe, seek, confess, ask, listen, trust, and have faith. We must do our part, so that God can do his.

Prayer

Our Father, which art in Heaven. *Thank you for being my stronghold – a place of safety and shelter when my life is disrupted by life's circumstances. Thank you knowing my heart when it cries out to you as you wrap me in in the comfort of your arms and your heart. Thank you for each opportunity to see your glory and your deliverance in my life. Lord, you have promised us peace, so we wait on you. We build our relationship and hope in you, while we wait. And, in our waiting is our journey toward learning and knowing your heart. Glory to your name. In Jesus' name we pray.* **Amen.**

Reflections

What / How are you hearing from God today?

What is your personal prayer for today?

"And he said: "The Lord is my rock and my fortress and my deliverer; The God of my strength, in whom I will trust; My shield and the horn of my salvation, My stronghold and my refuge; My Savior, You save me from violence. I will call upon the Lord, who is worthy to be praised; So shall I be saved from my enemies."

II Samuel 22:2-4 NKJV

Prayers of Healing and Moving Forward

Heavenly Father, *thank you for all things. Father, as we end our period of reflection and fasting, please continue to help us see those things in our lives that hold us back. Guide us to know that with you, our God, we can begin to break the barriers and strongholds of our lives. Father, guide our hearts and minds so that every thought is guided by the love of Christ. Father, we have many strongholds and distractions in our lives that desire to conquer us and separate us from you. We ask that you bind those actions and bring us into alignment with your will for our lives. In Jesus' name, we pray.* *Amen.*

Our Father, *hallowed be thy name. Father, thank you for these days of the fast. Thank you for whispering to us during this time. Help us to remember these lessons throughout the rest of this year. Help us to recall the revelations and your whispers of comfort, as we continue to grow stronger, closer to you, and release the ties that bind. In Jesus' name we pray and praise you in advance.* *Amen.*

Epilogue - Post Reflection

As I write this, I am reminded that - yes - God can zap our troubles away at any moment. But will we appreciate the immediate deliverance as much if we don't do the work? Being a part of our personal deliverance allows us to help ourselves, learn more about ourselves, and strengthen ourselves; so that we can also help others as we participate in the building of God's Kingdom.

The more we study, the more we feel his presence. The more we pray, the more we hear the whispers of his heart. The more we strive toward God, the more we see him and his love in all aspects of our lives.

Father, *remind us that all struggles are not meant to break us. Teach us to learn to grow stronger in Faith and in You. Thank you, Lord, on this journey to place our strongholds into obedience of Christ.* **Glory to God. Amen.**

Word for the Road, Amen

"The Lord is my light and my salvation; Whom shall I fear?
The Lord is the strength of my life; Of whom shall I be afraid?"

Psalm 27:1 NKJV

"Therefore, if anyone is in Christ, he is a new creation; old
things have passed away; behold, all things have become new.

II Corinthians 5:17 NKJV

"Do not lie to one another, since you have put off the old man
with his deeds, and have put on the new man who is renewed
in knowledge according to the image of Him who created him,

Colossians 3:9-10 NKJV

Three Prayers for the Road

Stand, Watch, Wait...

*"I will stand my **watch** And set myself on the rampart, And **watch to see** what He will say to me, And what I will answer when I am corrected."*

Habakkuk 2:1 NKJV

*"I will climb up to my **watch**tower and stand at my guardpost. There I will **wait** to see what the Lord says and how he will **answer** my complaint."*

Habakkuk 2:1 NLT

I.

Heavenly Father, thank you for all things. Father, please, grant us the strength to stand and the courage to wait. Grant us listening ears and hearing hearts. Open our natural eyes and our spiritual eyes so that we may see what you have in store for us. We seek you in prayer. We look for you in the whispers and in the wind. We long to hear from you and we are listening, watching, and waiting for you. In Jesus' name, we pray. *Amen.*

II.

Father God, close my mouth and open my heart to hear. So often, we begin listening and offering our explanations at the same time - before we hear all there is to be said. Father, give us a pause in our response so that we may hear all of what you have to say to us, all of your guidance - before we choose to act or respond. Grant us, we pray, the patience to be quiet and listen. In Jesus' name, we pray. *Amen.*

III.

Gracious Lord, Scripture states watch to see your answer. Father, sometimes we are so busy looking, we cannot see what is right in front of us. Remind us, Lord, to breathe and focus. Focus on you. Focus on seeking the path you have for us. Focus on the natural beauty of life – relationships, nature, and _____. Father, as we wait for your answer, grant us patience so that we do not move too soon or too late. Father, we know that you will answer, because you have promised. My Lord, we need to hear from you. In Jesus' name we pray. *Amen.*

What Is Your Prayer?

Benediction

"Be anxious for nothing, but in everything by prayer and supplication, with thanksgiving, let your requests be made known to God; and the peace of God, which surpasses all understanding, will guard your hearts and minds through Christ Jesus."

Philippians 4:6-7 NKJV

"Now may the God of hope fill you with all joy and peace in believing, that you may abound in hope by the power of the Holy Spirit."

Romans 15:13 NKJV

"Oh, magnify the Lord with me, And let us exalt His name together. I sought the Lord, and He heard me, And delivered me from all my fears."

Psalm 34:3-4 NKJV

Thoughts, Prayers, Reflections

_____

_____

_____

_____

_____

_____

_____

_____

_____

_____

_____

_____

_____

_____

_____

_____

_____

_____

_____

_____

Thoughts, Prayers, Reflections

_____

_____

_____

_____

_____

_____

_____

_____

_____

_____

_____

_____

_____

_____

_____

_____

_____

_____

_____

Thoughts, Prayers, Reflections

_____

_____

_____

_____

_____

_____

_____

_____

_____

_____

_____

_____

_____

_____

_____

_____

_____

_____

Additional Author's Works

Why Should I Be Bound? Musings on a Journey with God (2018)

Pray, Praise and Be Encouraged - A 21-day devotional (2020)

Prayers for a Friend (2021)

Moments of Grace: A New Beginning (2023)

Walking With Gace: A Fresh Start (2023)

Sufficient Grace: New Mercies Each Day (2023)

Prayers for the Journey (2023)

Prayers for your Fasting Journey (2024)

Praying Through The Psalms (2025)

To purchase visit:

www.vernetcnettles.com

www.amazon.com

About the Author

Vernet Clemons Nettles, EdD is a parent, retired educator, speaker and writing coach. Throughout the years, she has served in various capacities of church service education administration.

Dr. Nettles enjoys seeking Christ, researching the Word of God, and relishing in the aha moments of God's promises.

Let's Stay Connected:

www.vernetcnettles.com

https://www.vernetcnettles.com/vcn-daily-pray.html

vernetcnettles@gmail.com

www.ingramcontent.com/pod-product-compliance
Lightning Source LLC
Chambersburg PA
CBHW070024110426
42741CB00034B/2490